Praise for the Budgetnista

Melissa Thanks again Tiffany TheBudgetnista! You SAVED my life literally! to some it's may be just money but everything was at stake for me. God bless you!!!

The Whole Woman Project shared your photo.
The Budgetnista is not just telling you how to get out of debt but she keeps it real about her getting out of debt. Love The Budgetnista.

Allison ▸ **Tiffany TheBudgetnista**
1 hr

Thanks Tiffany TheBudgetnista you make budgeting and saving so much fun. ☺

Lauren Lol! Tiffany TheBudgetnista, you really have no clue how many times a day your name, or the name of your group is mentioned in this household! You have truly changed the way the hubby and I look at money and credit! I thank you and I hope that people don't scroll past this post but instead actually get involved and get right! ☺

Maya @Educ8Money2Kids · 12m
Love how @TheBudgetnista defines money. Money is a tool. It can be used to build or destroy your financial life. YOU determine how it's used

Rachel @TheBelleAgency · 27 Dec
Was able to lower my car insurance today after going deeper into @TheBudgetnista's book. Y'all are sleeping if you haven't gotten it yet.

Praise for the Budgetnista

Lorraine 23 hours ago `LINKED COMMENT`
Oh my gosh! I think you are wonderful!! Come Jan 1 I'm planning on paying down my debt!! You came along at a PERFECT time! Your plan makes so much sense! Your book is on its way!! You are a God send!! I'll keep in touch to let you know how it's going. While waiting for the book I'll be watching your YouTube videos! I'm so excited!!! Thank you for sharing your knowledge! ~Lorraine

Radiant Yes ! Yes! Tiffany TheBudgetnista is defying all types of gender bias, stereotypes, and shattering glass ceilings in the financial advising profession! She getting all bicostal, cross-gender, and multi-socioeconomic..Go head Tiff!!!

Side note: I sincerely appreciate this awe-inspiring group of individuals. ((((Virtual Hugs))))

Elizabeth
Today I took the first step in living the way I would like instead of waiting for the lottery to bless me I was able to make a sizeable donation to a friend's business, and I couldn't stop talking about how you helped make it possible, Tiffany TheBudgetnista Aliche! One of my goals this year is to support projects that help us grow as a community. Some people think I have a lot of money, but a little bit at a time adds up to something great!

Like · Comment · Stop Notifications · 3 hours ago via mobile

Latrice Tiffany TheBudgetnista, I just finished listening to your podcast interview and it is inspiring to know that someone just like everyone else has experienced financial hardships that are relatable to ours and is not judgemental; but enjoy sharing your wealth of information to help the rest of us to live or best lives. Thanks!

Praise for the Live Richer Challenge

Khalilah ⬛⬛⬛⬛ Keep me posted Tiffany TheBudgetnista if they want someone on the East Coast! The whole challenge was a huge blessing for me! The biggest benefit I received from the challenge is a new mindset. My thinking has totally been transformed as a result of the LRC. That is priceless and something that can never be taken away from me!!! #Blessed and thanks again Tiffany for the passionate work that you do!

1 min · Unlike · 👍 1

Chiniqua ⬛⬛⬛ ▸ Dream Catchers : LIVE RICHER
16 hrs

I've been in this group for a while and never posted anything. Just wanted to share a little today. Before I started the challenge I had a maxed out credit card, all of my bills were past due, I had multiple pay day loans, and a credit score in the 400s. I had a shopping problem and continued to shop and waste money knowing my bills weren't paid. Sometimes I had to borrow money from my mother to get to work. It took an eviction notice and my cable getting cut off for me to wake up.

I found the challenge and it really helped me to get my priorities straight. It took a lot of hard work. I had to cut everything that was not necessary out of my budget. No shopping trips. No spending $15 a day eating out. No buying expensive gifts. I learned to do my own hair and nails. I bring my lunch everyday. I learned how to coupon and actually enjoy being cheap.

I'm finally caught up on all my bills, credit card is paid off, and I even opened my first savings account. It feels so good knowing I don't owe money to anyone and have a little nest egg. Thanks Tiffany for creating the challenge and everyone in the group for all the great advice you post. 😊

LIVE RICHER CHALLENGE. Copyright © 2014

The Budgetnista and its logo, $B, are trademarks of Tiffany Aliche

No part of this book may be reproduced or transmitted in any form or by any means, electronic or mechanically, including photocopying, recording, or by any information storage and retrieval system, without written permission from the publisher. For more information, contact Tiffany Aliche at tiffany@thebudgetnista.com.

Disclaimer:
This book is designed to provide accurate and reliable information on the subject of personal finance. This book is sold with the understanding that neither the author nor the publisher is engaged in representation of legal, accounting or other professional services by publishing this book. As each individual situation is unique, questions relevant to personal finance and specific to the individual should be addressed to an appropriate professional. Doing so ensures that the particular situation has been evaluated professionally, carefully and properly. The author and publisher specifically disclaim any liability, loss, or risk that is incurred as an outcome, directly or indirectly, through the use and application of any contents of this work.

Visit the website:
www.thebudgetnista.com

To The Budgetnista Team.
Thank you for helping me to create a movement that has helped so many.

– Live Richer

Tiffany

Let's get to know each other.

Hi, I'm Tiffany. Welcome to the beginning of your savings journey! If you're ready to fix your credit and live a more abundant life, you've come to the right place.

To LIVE RICHER means to purposefully and passionately design the life you deserve. The purpose of the *LIVE RICHER Challenge: Credit Edition* is to teach you how to raise your credit score and clean up your credit report so you can lead the life you desire.

Although I received a financial education growing up, I haven't always made the best money choices. I love to share my story because it proves that no matter how bad a situation may seem, it's possible to dig your way out.

Tiffany's Financial Fiascos

1. At age 24, I took a $20,000 cash advance from my credit card and invested it with a "friend". This genius move landed me in $35,000 worth of debt a few months later.

2. At age 26, I bought my first home—right before the housing bubble burst. The value of my $220,000 condo declined to $150,000 during the Great Recession.

3. At age 30, as a result of losing my job during the Recession and being unable to keep up with my bills, the 802 credit score I once enjoyed quickly plummeted to 574.

Pretty bad, huh? Once I adopted my LIVE RICHER lifestyle, I was able to pay off my credit card debt in two and a half years, make peace with my mortgage lender, and raise my credit score almost 200 points in two years. I've even been able to travel to over 20 countries within the last few years.

Now, I use the solutions that helped me during my Financial Fiascos as a tool to guide people like you, who want to do the same.

In 2008, I started The Budgetnista, an award-winning professional and educational services firm. As "The Budgetnista", I'm a spokesperson—I also speak, write, teach and create financial education products and services that include seminars, workshops, curricula, and trainings.

I've written a bestselling book, *The One Week Budget* (a #1 Amazon bestseller), which teaches readers how to budget their income and automate the process over a period of just seven days. In 2015, I launched the first edition of the LIVE RICHER Challenge (you are currently reading the 3rd book in this series), which helped over 205,000 women across the world save Millions and pay off over hundreds of thousands worth of debt. I also wrote another #1 Amazon Bestseller called the *LIVE RICHER Challenge.* The book you're reading now is the **third** in my LIVE RICHER series.

You can learn more about me and The Budgetnista at www.thebudgetnista.com.

Why do this challenge?

Enough about me. Let's talk about you. Have you ever asked yourself any of these questions?

1. How is my credit score calculated?
2. How can I raise my credit score?
3. How can I clean-up my credit report?
4. How can I use credit as a tool to do the things I desire in life?

If so, great! This challenge will answer all of these questions, plus more! I even promise to do so in a straightforward way that'll be easy for you to implement. In just 22 days, you'll have a plan to accomplish your credit goals.

HOW TO READ THIS BOOK

Are you ready to fix your credit like a pro? Good, let's get to work.

How it works:
Each day I'll assign an Easy Financial Task designed to help you get and stay on the road to credit success.

The daily tasks will focus on the money theme of the week. The weekly themes for the LIVE RICHER Challenge: Credit Edition are:

Week 1: Credit Knowledge
Week 2: Credit Improvement
Week 3: Credit Maintenance
Final Day: LIVE RICHER

How to guarantee your success:
- Every morning, read and commit to the Easy Financial Task.

- Perform the task. Don't worry; it won't be hard.

- Get an accountability partner(s). The best way to rock this challenge is to partner up with at least one other person and work together. It'll keep you motivated. You can also reach out to and work with other Dream Catchers (the name I've given to folks working on the Challenge), in the private, Dream Catcher's LIVE RICHER **group** at www.livericherchallenge.com

- Share your experiences with me, ask questions, and leave comments via social media. You can find me online here:

The Budgetnista Blog: thebudgetnistablog.com
Twitter & Instagram: @TheBudgetnista
Facebook: The Budgetnista
I have also created many awesome resources for you that can't fit into this book. You can also find them for *free* at www.livericherchallenge.com.

LIVE RICHER,
Tiffany "The Budgetnista" Aliche

Table of Contents

Let's get to know each other 8

How to Read This Book 10

Week 1: Credit Knowledge

Credit Knowledge Week Goals 15
Day 1: Credit Goals 16
Day 2. Credit Basics 19
Day 3. Grab Free Credit Reports 23
Day 4. Grab Free Credit Scores 25
Day 5. Credit Score Calculations 28
Day 6. Review, Reflect, Relax 32
Day 7. Weekly Inspiration 33

Week 2: Credit Improvement

Credit Improvement Week Goals 35
Day 8. Credit Report Clean Up 36
Day 9. Bills on Lock 41
Day 10. Amounts Owed 44
Day 11. Length of Credit History 50
Day 12. 100 points 54
Day 13. Review, Reflect, Relax 56
Day 14. Weekly Inspiration 57

Week 3: Credit Maintenance

Credit Maintenance Week Goal 59
Day 15. Hard vs. Soft Inquiry 60
Day 16. Your Credit Mix 63
Day 17. Lower Interest Rates 67
Day 18. Relationships and Credit 71
Day 19. Scams and Fraud 76
Day 20. Review, Reflect, Relax 80
Day 21. Weekly Inspiration 81

LIVE RICHER

Live Richer Goal: 82
Day 22: LIVE RICHER 83

WEEK 1: CREDIT KNOWLEDGE

THIS WEEK'S GOAL:

To learn what credit is, how to get your credit report for free, and how areas of your credit report impact your credit score.

Live Richer Challenge: Credit Edition
Day 1: Credit Goals

Week 1: Credit Knowledge

Today's Easy Financial Task: Identify, write down, and share your credit goals.

How to rock this task:
- List up to two specific goals for your credit
- Write down your goal(s)
- Share them (tell me, tell a friend, or share your goals in the Dream Catcher Facebook Group)

Welcome to the the first week of the Live Richer Challenge: Credit Edition. Woot! Woot!

Our mission this week is to tackle the fundamentals of credit including what's on your credit report and how your credit report is used to calculate your credit score. A solid understanding of these basics is what will help you achieve long-term credit score growth and maintenance.

Are you excited?! I am!

On the first day of each Live Richer Challenge, we tackle our goals. The Credit Edition is no different. Let's get started.

I want you to identify two specific credit goals you want to work on during this Challenge, and what goals you want to continue working on after this Challenge comes to a close.

Know this: your credit score may not improve by leaps and bounds overnight, or within the three weeks of this Challenge. Buuuuut, making a commitment to do what's necessary to improve your credit long-term will produce the results you desire.

Take me for example. I was able to increase my credit score by over 200 points (from 547 to 750) in a year and a half. It's possible folks!

Make sure you write down when and how you plan to achieve your credit goals.

Not sure how to make your credit goal(s) happen? Don't worry!

Next week, I'll be giving you tasks to work on that will help you clean up your credit report and increase your credit score. You can always update your "how" as we move forward with the Challenge.

Next, write down your goals and post them somewhere.

I created a credit, goal sheet for you. You can find this free resource at www.livericherchallenge.com under the book resources tab (Day 1: Credit Goals).

Don't forget, you need to pick an accountability partner(s).

I suggest picking a friend or organizing a group of people who want to do the Challenge with you, so you're both on the same page.

You can also head into the Dream Catcher Facebook Group to find other Dream Catchers who are working through the Challenge as well. Send a request to get into the group at www.livericherchallenge.com.

If you have any questions, you can reach out to me on social media here:

Twitter: @thebudgetnista
Instagram: @thebudgetnista
Facebook: The Budgetnista

Private Forum: www.livericherchallenge.com (Go to the website and request to join the private LIVE RICHER forum.)

I can't wait to hear what you'll be working on!

My credit goals are...

- To reach a credit score of 800
- To close all collections
- Pay off all credit card debt down to 30% and under utilization
- Pay off student loan

Live Richer Challenge: Credit Edition
Day 2: Credit Basics

Week 1: Credit Knowledge

Today's Easy Financial Task: Learn about credit and your credit report.

How to rock this task:
- Learn about credit
- Learn the purpose of a credit report

You've made it to the second day of the Challenge. Woot, woot!

Today we're going to dive into credit basics including what credit is and why it's important. We'll also discuss what a credit report is. Let's get to it!

What is Credit?

There are two definitions of credit.

When an entity offers you a product or service that you agree to pay for later, they're offering you this product or service on "credit." In this case, credit is the promise or "IOU" with the understanding that you will pay later.

The second definition of credit is how good (or bad) you are at keeping the above promise. If you have "good credit," it means you're generally good at sticking to the agreement of paying your debts.

What Is A Credit Report?

A credit report is a detailed record of your financial history (like your ability to repay debt on time) and public records. It's like your "money report card."

Credit bureaus store financial data about us in huge databases. The financial information in the databases comes from data reported to the bureaus by our creditors.

When we (or other entities) search for our name, address, and social security number within the database, it pulls information about us and compiles it into an easy-to-read report.

The final product is (drum roll) your **credit report.** You can jump ahead of tomorrow's task and get your FREE report here: www.annualcreditreport.com.

Items that appear on your credit report include:
- Personal information like your social security number, address, date of birth, and employer
- Open and closed accounts including credit cards, mortgages, loans, etc. and the payment history on each account
- Public records like bankruptcies, liens, or judgements and accounts in collections
- Credit checks (also called credit inquiries) from lenders, employers, and other companies that you give authorization to check your credit report

The Three Credit Reporting Agencies
There are hundreds of different credit reporting agencies that collect information about us, but there are three major ones: Equifax, Experian, and TransUnion.

These three bureaus collect financial data and sell the information to other entities, including us. The information is sold to us if we sign up for services like identity theft or credit monitoring.

Here's a tool I recommend: Credit Sesame. Yes! Currently, when you sign up for Credit Sesame's free credit monitoring, they'll automatically give you **$50,000 worth of identity theft insurance, plus live access to talk to identity restoration specialists —** *for freeeeeeee.* In the event you are ever a victim of identity theft, you won't be alone to deal with it (like Superman), because they've got you covered.

> Superman's (my boo's) identity was stolen and it resulted in someone buying a car in his name, running tolls, lights and eventually a car accident. He had to go to court four times as a result. Yikes!
>
> He signed up for an Identity Theft service and it stopped instantly. It's worth it.

Protect yourself and your credit by using our special Dream Catcher link to sign-up for Credit Sesame at www.livericherchallenge.com, under the book resources tab (Day 2: Credit Basics).

Back to who gets your financial information...

Your information is also sold to creditors for their review when you apply for credit. (In order for these creditors to check your report, they must get your authorization. A credit check results in a credit inquiry on your report. We'll talk about the impact of inquiries on your credit report on Day 4 of this Challenge.)

Since there are three main credit bureaus, you also have three credit reports; one from each reporting agency. Why?

Although most of the information on your credit reports will be similar, there may be some small differences. This is primarily because creditors are not required to report your credit history to all three of the credit reporting agencies.

They may report to one, two, or none at all!

Why Credit and Your Credit Report is so Important

Financial institutions, employers, telephone providers, and other companies review the information on your credit reports to determine your creditworthiness.

Creditworthiness is an evaluation of how likely you are to repay debt in the future. Creditors make a judgment about your creditworthiness by reviewing items on your reports like your payment history and the amount of debt you have. Based on this judgment, they decide whether or not to extend you credit and at what interest rate.

Keeping your credit report void of negative records like late payments and unpaid balances is important because poor financial history can hold you back from qualifying for a low interest rate or qualifying for forms of credit at all.

Why Credit Isn't All Bad

Let's address the elephant in the room: credit is a form of debt.

Usually, when we talk of debt, we think bad news.

However, using debt responsibly isn't always negative. For example, buying a home with a home loan can be a worthwhile investment.

You need a positive credit history to qualify for that home loan.

You need to use credit responsibly to establish that positive credit history.

Don't worry, I'll show you how during this Challenge.

That's it for today Dream Catcher!

We covered a lot of information, so feel free to reach out if you have any questions.

Remember to reach out to your accountability partners to encourage each other through the Challenge. Check into the Dream Catchers: LIVE RICHER group as well.

Today I learned something new about credit. I learned that...

— Creditors are not required to report to all 3

Live Richer Challenge: Credit Edition
Day 3: Grab Free Credit Reports

Week 1: Credit Knowledge

Today's Easy Financial Task: Get your free credit report(s)

How to rock this task:
- Watch the video
- Go to www.experian.com, www.transunion.com, and www.equifax.com, or www.annualcreditreport.com, to get your free credit report
- Download the free Credit Score Explainer from MagnifyMoney

Hey there Dream Catchers! It's Day 3 of the Challenge. Guess what?

Once a week during the Challenge, I'll bring the daily task to you through a video.

Take a moment to watch the video at www.livericherchallenge.com under the book resources tab (Day 3, Grab Free Credit Reports).

Today is all about getting your credit report(s) for free and knowing how to read your credit report(s).

Remember, you have three credit reports because there are three different major credit reporting agencies - Experian, Equifax, and TransUnion.

How to Grab Your Free Credit Report(s)
Each of the credit bureaus allows you to get *one free* credit report every 12 months. You can get your reports all at once, or you can space them out throughout the year.

To pull your credit report, you can contact each credit bureau here:
- Experian: 1-888-397-3742 / www.experian.com
- TransUnion: 1-800-888-4213 / www.transunion.com
- Equifax: 1-800-685-1111 / www.equifax.com

You can also get it through one of my favorite sites, www.annualcreditreport.com. What I like about this site is that not only do you get your credit report for free, they teach you how to read, improve and maintain it for free too! It will not ask for your credit card. It will ask you to verify information that only you know about. Make sure you have access to a printer so you can print each one or save as a .pdf to access it later.

Yesterday, we went through an overview of the information that appears on your credit report.

Today, I have a super awesome downloadable Credit Score Explainer from MagnifyMoney that, along with the video, can assist you in reading the credit report you pull from today's task.

Get the free downloadable at www.livericherchallenge.com, under the book resources tab (Day 3, Grab Free Credit Reports).

If after reading your credit report you find errors or incomplete records, don't be alarmed!

We will discuss how to clean up your credit report next week.

Errors I found on my credit reports...

_____

_____

_____

_____

_____

_____

_____

Live Richer Challenge: Credit Edition
Day 4: Grab Free Credit Scores

Week 1: Credit Knowledge

Today's Easy Financial Task: Get your free credit score

How to rock this task:
- Learn what a credit score is
- Learn how to pull your credit score(s) for free

"Another day, another dollar." Or in this case, another day, another credit task.

Today's task is all about discussing what a credit score is and how to get access to your credit score(s) for free.

What's a credit score?

Don't confuse your credit score with your credit report.

The data on each of your credit reports is analyzed to assign you a credit score that reflects your risk.

A *high* credit score means you're a *lower* risk borrower who is likely to repay debt.

A *low* credit score means you're a *higher* risk borrower that may not be able to repay debt.

Since you have three different credit reports from each major credit bureau, you also have three different credit scores. Depending on where you pull your credit score, you may be able to get credit scores that reflect data from one, two, or all three of the bureaus.

There are several credit score grading systems, including consumer education scores offered by Experian, TransUnion, and Equifax. The purpose of consumer education scores are to give us a general sense of where we stand.

These scores are not typically used by the financial industry to make credit decisions.

The FICO Score Model

The top tier credit score model that's most often used by creditors to judge your creditworthiness is the FICO score model. This is the model we'll go over in this Challenge since it's the most widely used version.

FICO scores range from 300 to 850:

- 751 – 850 - Excellent
- 701 – 750 - Good
- 641 – 700 - Fair
- 581 – 641 - Poor
- 300 – 580 - Very Poor

Usually, you have to pay for a FICO score, but you can get access to comparable credit scores like the VantageScore for free.

The VantageScore uses a similar system as the FICO score model to arrive at your score and is a valuable way to measure your score growth. We'll talk about the factors that go into calculating your credit scores tomorrow.

Dream Catcher, you know I have a special place in my heart for you, so I found a place where you can get your FICO score for free. Yes, FREE!

How to Grab Your Free Credit Score(s)

You can hop on over to www.creditscorecard.com to get your FICO credit score for free.

You can also check with your bank or credit card company to see if free credit scores are offered to customers. For example, currently American Express, Bank of America, and Chase all offer free FICO scores if you have certain products.

Once you grab your credit score(s), take a moment to review them.

If you're shocked or worried about your score, don't fret.

During this Challenge, I'm going to give you tips to clean up your credit report and show you how you can increase your score by as much as 100 points in a year.

Reach out to your accountability partners and don't forget to check in with the Dream Catchers in the Dream Catchers: LIVE RICHER group as well.

My credit scores are:

Score: __625__ From __Credit Karma__ Date __6/14/20__

Score: __619__ From __discover__ Date __6/14/20__

Score: _____ From _____ Date _____

Score: _____ From _____ Date _____

Score: _____ From _____ Date _____

Score: _____ From _____ Date _____

Score: _____ From _____ Date _____

Live Richer Challenge: Credit Edition
Day 5: Credit Score Calculations

Week 1: Credit Knowledge

Today's Easy Financial Task: Learn how your credit score is calculated.

How to rock this task:
- Learn how your credit score is calculated
- Download Credit Score Decoded from MagnifyMoney

Woot, woot! Day 5, friends!

Today's an important day. We're diving into the factors that affect your credit score.

In total, there are five areas of your credit history that are used to calculate your credit score. Some components are more impactful to your score than others.

What's the purpose of this task?

In order to increase your credit score, you will need to identify the factors from your credit history that are hurting your score so you can make improvements.

So, let's get started!

The five factors used to calculate your credit score include:

- Payment history: 35% of your score
- Amounts owed: 30% of your score
- Length of credit history: 15% of your score
- Type of debt: 10% of your score
- Inquiries: 10% of your score

Let's break down the importance of each one:
Payment History (35% of Your Score)

Of all of the components, this one is the most influential. Your ability to pay your current bills on time is a good indicator of whether you'll be able to pay bills on time in the future. Late payments make you appear less creditworthy and, as a result, can do quite a bit of damage to your score.

Amounts Owed (30% of Your Score)

Amounts owed is how much debt you're carrying. Having a high amount of debt owed could mean you're having trouble paying your bills and is another red flag for companies measuring your creditworthiness.

There are three key factors that go into determining your mark in the amounts owed category including your credit utilization, amounts owed on installment loans, and overall balances.

Let's discuss each one in detail:
Credit Utilization

Your credit utilization is how much credit you're using on revolving accounts. Revolving accounts are credit lines that you can keep a revolving balance on from month-to-month like your credit card. To calculate your utilization, you:

- Add up the credit limits on your accounts
- Add up the balances on your accounts
- Divide your balance by your credit limit
- Multiply by 100

For example, if you have a credit card limit of $1,000 and your balance is $500, you're utilizing 50% of your available revolving credit.

Here's another example: Say you have two credit cards and each one has a $1,000 credit limit (that's a $2,000 credit limit in total). If one card is maxed out with a $1,000 balance and the other one has a zero balance, your credit utilization is also 50%. $2,000 credit limit / $1,000 balance x 100% = 50%

Your goal is to keep utilization at 30%, but even lower is better.

How Much You Owe On Installment Loans

An installment loan is a loan that has a set amount of payments and a set loan term. Examples include your mortgage and auto loans. Having less owed on your installment loans has a positive effect on your amounts owed.

How Many Revolving Accounts You Have With Balances or Have Maxed Out

Finally, the amount of revolving accounts (i.e. credit cards) that you have with a balance, or have maxed out the credit limit, will have an impact on your mark in the amounts owed category.

Length of Credit History (15% of Your Score)

The longer your credit history the better. Your credit card history is calculated using an average.

Here's an example: If you've had a mortgage for 15 years, a credit card for 10 years, and another credit card for two years, the length of your credit history equals nine years.

Keep this in mind before you close any of your accounts. Even if you pay off an account, closing it can significantly shorten your average history.

You also want to be careful of adding new accounts. From our example, you can see how the card that's only two years old has shortened the average history length. The average credit history would be three and a half years longer without that credit card.

Installment loans are treated differently than your revolving credit (i.e. credit cards). When you pay off a loan, the account is closed and no longer appears on your credit.

Type of Debt (10% of Your Score)

We've touched on the many types of debt you can have so far. A few examples being, credit cards, mortgages, auto loans, and personal loans.

Having a mix of accounts that are in good standing shows that you can manage various forms of debt responsibly which can have a positive impact on your score.

Credit Inquiries (10% of Your Score)

A credit inquiry is when someone you authorize to look up your credit does a credit check. Too many credit inquiries can ding your credit score a few points and stay on your report for two years. Be cautious with who you allow to check your report.

It's Time for Review

Now that we've covered the five components of your score, dig into your credit report(s) to see where you stand with each one.

Take out a highlighter or pen and note the positive and negative. We'll circle back on how you can make improvements in the areas you circle next week.

As a supplement to the FICO score overview in this task, I've provided you with another awesome download from MagnifyMoney that goes even further into detail about how your credit score works. Get this free download at www.livericherchallenge.com under the book resources tab (Day 5, Credit Score Calculations.)

That's all for Day 5, Dream Catchers!

Tomorrow is a day to review the tasks from the last five days.

Live Richer Challenge: Credit Edition
Day 6: Review, Reflect, Relax

Week 1: Credit Knowledge

Today's Easy Financial Task: Review, Reflect, Relax

How to rock this task:
- Review this week's Live Richer Challenge: Credit Edition tasks
- Reflect on the credit basics and the components that make up your credit score
- Relax. In two days we start Week 2: Credit Improvement
  Round of applause!

You've completed the first week of the Live Richer Challenge: Credit Edition. Woo hoo!

Take this day to review, reflect, and relax.

Today is a great day to check in on your accountability partner. Do they need help with a task? Do they need some encouragement? Be sure to reach out!

I'd love to hear from you too. You can reach out to me here:

Twitter: @thebudgetnista
Instagram: @thebudgetnista
Facebook: The Budgetnista
Private Forum: www.livericherchallenge.com
(Go to the website and request to join the private LIVE RICHER forum.

Don't forget: It's great to be helped, but it's even greater to use what you've been given to help someone else. Share the wealth and pass the Live Richer Challenge: Credit Edition along to someone you know who is struggling to get their credit on track.

Live Richer Challenge: Credit Edition
Day 7: Weekly Inspiration

Week 1: Credit Knowledge

Today's Easy Financial Task: Watch the Week 1 Dream Catcher Hangout Chat.

How to rock this task:
- Watch the chat & participate if watching live.
- Listen to words of encouragement.
- Complete Challenge tasks you missed.

Today's our first Dream Catcher Hangout video!

During the video, we discuss the tasks we've worked on this week. We'll also talk about the key takeaways and you'll hear how other Dream Catchers like yourself are working through the Challenge.

Make sure to check in on your accountability partner. Have they completed the first week of the Challenge? Are they ready for next week?

FYI: Today is a good day to catch up on any tasks that you missed throughout the week. (Make sure you've pulled your free credit reports and scores because you'll need it for future Challenge days.) Tomorrow we have a fresh new week full of tasks to help you improve your credit score!

Watch the Dream Catcher Hangout at www.livericherchallenge.com under the book resources tab, (Day 7: Weekly Inspiration)

Week 1: Credit Mindset Recap Checklist

This Week's Goal: To learn what credit is, how to get your credit report for free, and how areas of your credit report impact your credit score.

- **Day 1:** Credit Goals
  - ○ Easy Financial Task: Identify, write down, and share your credit goals.
- **Day 2:** Credit Basics
  - ○ Easy Financial Task: Learn about credit and your credit report.
- **Day 3:** Grab Free Credit Reports
  - ○ Easy Financial Task: Get your free credit report(s).
- **Day 4:** Grab Free Credit Scores
  - ○ Easy Financial Task: Get your free credit score
- **Day 5:** Credit Score Calculations
  - ○ Easy Financial Task: Learn how your credit score is calculated.
- **Day 6:** Review, Reflect, Relax
  - ○ Easy Financial Task: Review, Reflect, Relax
- **Day 7:** Weekly Inspiration
  - ○ Easy Financial Task: Watch the Week 1 Dream Catcher Hangout Chat.

Week 1 Reflections

_____

_____

_____

_____

_____

_____

_____

_____

_____

WEEK 2: CREDIT IMPROVEMENT

THIS WEEK'S GOAL:

To raise your credit score

Live Richer Challenge: Credit Edition
Day 8: Credit Report Clean Up

Week 2: Credit Improvement

Today's Easy Financial Task: To identify items on your credit report you can dispute.

How to rock this task:
- Review each item on your credit report for accuracy
- Identify errors, incomplete records, and items you can dispute
- File a dispute
- Get your free Credit Repair Guide from MagnifyMoney

Welcome to Week 2 of the LRC: Credit Challenge! How are you feeling, Dream Catcher?

Are you ready to dig in?

Let's get to it!

This week is going to be jam-packed with tasks that will set you on the path to improving your credit score and report. For today's task, we're going to clean up your credit report by identifying incorrect items that you should dispute.

There are several reasons why there could be errors or incomplete records on your report. Sometimes mistakes happen when inputting the personal information, payment history, and account data on your report, or account updates (like an acknowledgement that you've settled a debt) aren't reported to the bureau(s).

Incorrect or incomplete information can have a negative impact on your score. We don't want that, my friend.

The good news is under the Fair Credit Reporting Act (FCRA) you have the right to dispute items on your report.

The reporting agency must respond to your disputes (unless frivolous) and provide verification of each record. If they can't verify the record it must be removed.

Yup, you've got some power here!

So, today I want to you dig into your credit report to locate items you can dispute. Then, I'll tell you step-by-step how to file a dispute.

First, pull out a pen and your free credit report(s) from Day 3's task.

Here's what you need to review on your credit report:

1. **Your personal information:** Check your name, address, and basic information to make sure they are all correct.

2. **Each of your accounts:** Scan the accounts carefully on your credit report to verify that what's being reported is accurate. Here are a few aspects of your accounts that you want to double-check:
   - The payment history on all accounts are correct and current
   - There are no accounts that don't belong to you
   - There are no old debts that appear unpaid that you've taken care of
   - The status of each account including the day you opened and/or closed the account is correct

3. **The age of any negative history:** After seven years, negative history like late payments should fall off of your credit report. If old negative history is still appearing on your account beyond 7 years, this is something you can dispute to have removed. Public records like bankruptcy, judgements, tax liens, or foreclosure can stay on your report for up to 10 years. Again, if you see a public record showing up beyond ten years, you have a right to dispute it.

4. **Your public record information (if applicable):** Check that your public records (tax liens, bankruptcies, or civil judgements) are accurate including the dates, courthouse, docket number, and status (paid or unpaid).

5. **Check the credit inquiries:** Make sure that in the hard credit inquiry section, that you gave each creditor listed permission to access your credit information.

If you find any items on your credit report that you need to dispute, circle them and then head on to the next step.

How to Dispute Errors

Here's how to dispute to clean up your report:

1. **Grab the mailing address:** Grab the address of the credit bureau you want to dispute your report with below:

Experian
Experian
P.O. Box 4500
Allen, TX 75013

Equifax
Equifax Information Services LLC
P.O. Box 740256
Atlanta, GA 30374

TransUnion
Consumer Dispute Center
P.O. Box 2000
Chester, PA 19016

2. **Gather proof:** Put together the evidence to send to the credit bureau. Include documents to prove your identity like a copy of your state issued ID, driver's license, or utility bill with your current address.

3. **State your case:** Write a letter to the bureau detailing the information you found that's incorrect and include your proof in the letter. Also, include a copy of your report with the errors marked.

4. **Send the letter through certified mail:** Make sure to request a return receipt. After you send in a letter, the creditor has to investigate the item(s) you found within 20 days unless your claim is found to be frivolous.

6. **Warning: Don't use the online dispute.** The online dispute option may have fine print that says you give up the right to re-dispute that claim if the bureau makes a decision that's not in your favor. You don't want to give up your right to dispute again if necessary.

If your request is approved...

The credit bureau will send you an updated copy of your credit report. You should also ask them to send a correction notice to anyone that's performed a credit check on you in the last six months.

Remember, you have three credit reports from three credit bureaus. If you found an error on one, you should check the others to make sure they're accurate as well.

If your request is denied...

Within 15 days of the date the investigation is concluded, the credit bureau has to show proof of the information from the company used to verify the item on your credit if you request it. If they cannot provide this information, the item has to be removed from your credit report.

This is all quite a bit of paperwork, so you should develop an organization system to keep track of your credit reports, the information to back up your dispute, and the date you need to request verification of the record.

Being persistent may cause them just to correct the information rather than jumping through the extra hoop of getting you the proof.

Bottom line: Don't give up!

Disputing Reports with Original Creditors and Collections Agencies

Both the bureaus *and* the entity that provides the data on your report are equally responsible for keeping it accurate. If you noticed an error, it's important to also resolve the error with the original creditor.

Call up the company that reported the error to the credit card bureaus to find out how you can file a dispute. Send the same proof that you send to the credit bureaus to the reporting entity.

Now, it's time to conquer this task! MagnifyMoney has a free Credit Report Guide to help you really rock this task. You can get it at www.livericherchallenge.com, under the book resources tab (Day 8: Credit Report Clean Up).

If you have any questions, reach out. Don't forget to keep tabs on your accountability partner(s)! Teamwork makes the dream work.

You can reach out to me here:

Twitter: @thebudgetnista
Instagram: @thebudgetnista
Facebook: The Budgetnista
Private Forum: www.livericherchallenge.com (Go to the website and request to join the LIVE RICHER forum by clicking the word "Forum".)

Errors I found on my credit reports...

_____

_____   _____

_____

_____

_____

Live Richer Challenge: Credit Edition
Day 9: "Bills on Lock"

Week 2: Credit Improvement

Today's Easy Financial Task: Automate your bill payments to improve your payment history record.

How to rock this task:
- Set up a separate account for your bills
- Automate bill payments from your bills account

On to the next day!

Today, we're going to talk about paying your bills on time. As we discussed last week, your ability to pay bills on time is the component of your credit history that holds the most weight when calculating your credit score.

Remember:
- Payment history: 35% of your score
- Amounts owed: 30% of your score
- Length of credit history: 15% of your score
- Type of debt: 10% of your score
- Inquiries: 10% of your score

If you've had a few slip ups in the past and not paid bills on time, don't feel bad.

As time passes, the recent history of paying on time will supersede past missed payments. Then, after seven years, late payments fall off of your credit report altogether.

The purpose of this task is to put in place a process that will help make sure you never make a late payment again.

Here's how to do it:

Open a Checking Account for Bills

Open up a new account at the same bank where you have your current checking account so you can easily transfer funds from one to the other. The new checking account will be specifically for bills. Make sure the checking account you open offers a bill pay service.

Do not connect a debit card to your bills account. (It's not a fallback account when you want to go shopping!)

Automate Your Bill Payments

Here's how to automate payments:

1. Tally up the total amount you pay on various bills.

2. Set up automatic transfers of that amount from your main checking account to your bills account.

3. Use the bill pay feature offered by your bank to send out automatic payments to cover your bills. There's a reason to use bill pay from your bank instead of setting up automatic payments with each company. You want to avoid putting your information in another company's system. Having your bank transfer money or write checks on your behalf is safer.

What About Past Due Accounts?

You may be thinking: getting your life together now is all well and good, what about fixing past mistakes?

Another way you can get a credit score boost is by bringing your past due accounts current. It's considered an "extra credit" on the FICO score metric.

So, if you do find yourself in a situation where you have some late payments on your report (that are accurate), you can turn the tide in your favor by making a change now. Then, use the tips above to make sure you don't fall back into the habit of paying late again.

That's it for today, Dream Catcher!

My monthly bills and their amounts…

Live Richer Challenge: Credit Edition
Day 10: Amounts Owed

Week 2: Credit Improvement

Easy Financial Task 11: Learn how to reduce the amount of debt you owe to improve your credit score.

How to Rock This Task:
- Review the amount of debt you owe in total (credit cards, auto loans, personal loans, mortgages, etc.)
- Use the debt snowball to reduce your debt
- Request a credit limit increase on your credit cards to reduce your credit utilization
- Apply for an installment loan to reduce your credit utilization

Welcome to Day 10 Dream Catcher! We're just about halfway through this Challenge. Woot, woot!

Yesterday, I gave you the method that I use to make sure my bills are always paid on time. Remember, paying your bills on time is the biggest part of your credit score, so it's something you want to be super vigilant about.

The amount of debt you owe is the next component that has the most weight on your credit score. For a quick recap:

- Payment history: 35% of your score
- Amounts owed: 30% of your score
- Length of credit history: 15% of your score
- Type of debt: 10% of your score
- Inquiries: 10% of your score

There are three factors that make up the amounts owed component of your score including your credit utilization, amount owed on installment loans, and your balances overall.

To improve the amounts owed portion of your score you can do these three things:
1. Pay off some of your debt (a.k.a. reduce the amount you owe)
2. Request a higher credit limit on your revolving accounts (i.e. credit cards) to reduce your credit utilization
3. Use an installment loan to pay off your revolving accounts

Let's cover them in detail.

Reduce the Amount You Owe

Lowering the amount of debt you owe may sound easier said than done, but I have a tactic you can use to get the ball rolling (pun intended) on your debt repayment plan.

It's called the debt snowball method!

The debt snowball is when you pay off debt from the smallest to largest balance. By default, your mortgage will likely be the debt you tackle last.

If you have credit card debt with high interest, you don't want to ignore it entirely while you repay other debt. So, next week, I'll teach you a few ways you can reduce interest rates on your revolving debt.

For now, let's focus in on setting up your debt repayment plan. Here's what to do:

1. List out all of your debt from lowest to highest balance.

2. Figure out how much money you can squeeze from your budget to put towards debt. Think about savings you can find from cutting excess. (If you need help coming up with a budget that will allow you to devote more money to debt, check out my bestselling book, The One Week Budget, available on Amazon)

3. Pay the minimum on all of your debt. Set up automatic payments to make the minimum payment on each debt.

4. **Pay the minimum and a little more on the smallest debt.** The debt that's at the top of your list should get more attention. Put any excess cash you can find in your budget towards this debt.

5. **Move on to the next debt on your list.** After you pay off the first debt, apply all the money you used each month to pay off the first debt towards the second debt on your list. This means the automated payment for your second debt should now include the minimum payment from your first. Put all excess money you can find from day-to-day towards the second debt as well.

6. **Keep the snowball rolling.** Once the second debt is paid off, follow the same cycle for the third. Automate the money that was going to the first and second debt to the third debt.

You should keep going with the debt snowball until it pays off all of your debt. You'll begin to see positive results in your credit score as your debt decreases.

Need more help? I've created a My Debt List spreadsheet that you can access for free at www.livericherchallenge.com under the book resources tab (Day 10: Amounts Owed). You can also find it at the end of today's task.

Request a Higher Credit Limit

To calculate your revolving credit utilization, you need to:

- Add up the credit limits on your revolving accounts
- Add up the balances on your revolving accounts
- Divide your balance by your credit limit
- Multiply by 100

You want your revolving credit utilization to stay below 30%. If your revolving credit utilization is above 30%, there are two variables you can change to lower it.

You can pay off some debt, which we discussed above, or you can ask your credit card company for a higher credit line.

To do this, pick your oldest card with the best payment history and call the customer service number on the back. Ask the customer service representative for a credit line increase.

You'll have the best bet at getting a credit limit increase approved on an account with good standing, but it doesn't hurt to ask. One thing to keep in mind is that a credit line increase may trigger a hard inquiry on your credit report which can impact you a few points.

Be sure to ask the customer service representative whether or not the increase will require a hard pull.

Pay Off Credit Card Debt With an Installment Loan

If you qualify for an installment or personal loan that has lower interest than your credit cards, using one can alleviate the debt that's calculated in your credit utilization to improve your score.

Remember, there's a difference between revolving debt (credit cards) and installment loans (i.e. personal loans, auto loans, and mortgages.)

Credit card debt is used to calculate your credit utilization which has the most impact on the Amounts Owed part of your score. If you transfer your credit card debt over to an installment loan, your scores will increase because your credit utilization will decrease.

The benefit of a personal loan is also twofold. Your credit utilization will decrease and you can get a lower interest rate with a personal loan saving you money.

Double whammy!

Here's how to find an installment loan:

1. Go to www.magnifymoney.com/shop/budgetnista to search for a personal loan that has low fees and a lower interest rate than your credit cards.

2. When you find a personal loan that has favorable terms, make sure you read the details and confirm:

   a. The loan interest rate
   b. How long the loan term is
   c. Whether applying for the loan will trigger a hard inquiry on your report (don't worry - none of the providers used in the tool with MagnifyMoney use a hard pull)
   d. If there are any fine print fees you should be aware of

Important Tip: Factors that determine the full cost of an installment loan include the interest rate, your monthly payment, *and* how long the loan term is.

Make sure to ask how much you'll pay in interest for the **entire** loan term to find an installment loan that will save you the most money.
Now, it's time to get to it.

First, follow the steps above to set up your debt repayment plan. Next, automate your minimum payments and focus in on repaying your smallest debt first.

Lastly, reach out to your credit card company to request a credit line increase or shop around for a personal loan to reduce your credit utilization.

That's it for Day 10 Dream Catcher!

Remember, if you need help during today's task reach out to your accountability partner(s).

My Debt List
(NOTE: List debt lowest to highest)

NAME OF DEBT	TOTAL AMT. OWED	MIN. MONTHLY PMT.	INTEREST RATE	DUE DATE	STATUS

Live Richer Challenge: Credit Edition
Day 11: Length of Credit History

Week 2: Credit Improvement

Today's Easy Financial Task: Learn strategies to lengthen your credit history.

How to rock this task:
- Find out what credit piggybacking is
- Review credit card and loan options for building credit

Day 11 Dream Catcher! Let's dig into today's task.

Today we're going to talk about your credit history length and how to improve it.

Building credit can be a catch-22. You need access to credit to build credit, but some companies are unwilling to give you a chance if you don't already have an established credit history.

Thankfully, there are a few ways to establish good credit history if you have little experience (or bad experience) using credit.

Credit Piggybacking

You may have heard of credit piggybacking before. It's when someone you know who has a credit card in excellent standing adds you as an authorized user on their account.

As an authorized user, you take on all the benefits of their positive payment history because the account will appear on your credit report. Here are some rules for choosing the right person to piggyback off of:

- The card you become an authorized user on should be at least three years old.
- The card should have a low balance.

- The card should have a perfect payment history.
- The card issuer should report authorized users to the credit bureaus, otherwise it's a waste of time. (You can check what bureau the card issuer reports to by giving them a call.)

The good news about credit piggybacking is that you're not responsible for the main account holder's debt. However, a word of warning is necessary here. If the account that you piggyback on goes unpaid, it can negatively impact your score.

Since you're not responsible for this debt, you can easily write into the creditor or credit bureau to have the account removed from your history.

Not just anyone with an excellent credit history is going to allow you to become an authorized user on their account, which is understandable. After all, they've put in the hard work building credit.

Who would want to risk someone coming along and racking up debt on their account as an authorized user?

Be mindful of this when asking someone to do you a favor. A parent, spouse, or close family member may be most willing to allow you to piggyback on their account. If friends and family are hesitant to add you as an authorized user out of fear you'll go crazy with the card, suggest they keep the card and restrict your access to the account.

Make sure they're also aware that your credit will not impact them when you're an authorized user. This may sway the decision in your favor.

Credit Cards for Building Credit

If you don't have access to someone that you can piggyback on to build your credit history, there are credit card options available to help you build credit as well.

For example, secured cards are cards that you can get approved for with no history or even poor history. A secured credit card is one where you put down a cash deposit (typically $200 to $500) which acts as your credit line.

Once you prove you can pay on time the deposit is eventually refunded, and the credit card issuer may increase your credit line.

To find the best secured cards:

1. Go to magnifymoney.com.
2. Search for secured cards.
3. Choose a secured card with no annual fee, a low interest rate, and a deposit amount you can manage.

If you're in school, college student cards are also available with lenient terms for those who are new to credit. Although, you do want to be careful.

If you're a student taking out a card, make sure you have the means to pay off the balance at the end of each statement period. Don't fall into the student credit card trap of using it to make all types of purchases that you can't pay off. Revolving a balance to the next month can get you caught in the "debt shuffle." You don't want that.

Check out this round up post on the best credit cards for college students at MagnifyMoney to choose a card at www.livericherchallenge.com, under the book resources tab (Day 11: Length of Credit History).

When shopping for a student card or secured card, there are some important things to watch out for. Check to make sure that:

1. The credit card issuer won't charge any crazy fees to start a credit card account.

2. The transactions and payment history on your credit card will be reported to all major credit bureaus. Your account activity being reported is what will help you build credit.

3. You're getting a secured card or student card with a company, credit union, or bank that you plan to stick around with for a little while. Eventually you may want to apply for a regular card.

Applying for a new card will count as a credit inquiry on your credit report and can stay on your report for two years. The inquiry may cause you to lose a few points on your credit score.

However, applying for a card to build credit can have benefits that will outweigh the brief dip in points. (We'll talk more about the two types of credit inquiries and how they impact your score next week.)

Using Credit Builder Loans

A credit builder loan is another way to establish credit. A credit builder loan is one that you don't get money from upfront. Instead, you have to pay off the entire balance of the loan first in increments. After paying off the loan, you get the lump sum of cash.

The purpose of a credit builder loan is to help people with no credit or poor credit prove that they're able to make regular payments. Credit unions often have credit builder loans. If you're a credit union member, reach out to customer service to find out whether this is a product you qualify for.

Self Lender is another lender that offers credit builder loans. If you qualify for a loan with Self Lender, the money is kept in an FDIC-insured CD account until you repay the debt.

A few things to note about this account:

- There's a $12 administrative fee to apply for this loan
- There's interest on the loan of up to 14.77% APR

Before applying for this loan make sure you understand the fine print. I wrote a full review of how Self Lender works on my blog. You can read it at www.livericherchallenge.com (Day 11: Length of Credit History)

A major part of building your credit history is the waiting game. Having a long credit history won't happen overnight, but piggybacking and using cards or loans meant for building credit can help you along the way.

That's it for today's task!

Don't forget to reach out to your accountability partner(s) for support.

Live Richer Challenge: Credit Edition
Day 12: 100 Points

Week 2: Credit Improvement

Today's Easy Financial Task: Learn how to make your score jump like Jordan.

How to rock this task:
- Watch the video
- Use the tips from the video to raise your credit score

Day 12 Dream Catcher! Today is possibly my favorite day of this Challenge.

Today, I'm going to show you one of my favorite tactics that (in combination with the other tactics we've discussed so far) can make your credit score jump like Jordan. In fact, adding this strategy to your toolbelt can raise your credit score as much as 100 points in a year.

Yup, you read that right. 100 points in a year, Dream Catcher!

Watch the video at www.livericherchallenge.com (Day 12: 100 Points).

Here's the video recap:

Auto-paying off a small debt to zero each month can do wonders for your credit score.

Here's how to do it:

1. **Take out a credit card with a $0 balance.** If you don't already have a credit card with a $0 balance, you can apply for a new card. Go to MagnifyMoney.com and search for a card that has no annual fee. Apply for a secured card if you can't qualify for a regular one. You can use the steps from Day 11's task to find a secured card.

Keep in mind if you apply for a card it will cause an inquiry on your report. The inquiry can stay on your report for up to two years. The long-term advantages of using this method will likely outweigh the disadvantage of losing a few points for a short time.

2. **Place a small bill on the credit card.** Take your new card (or existing card with a $0 balance) and put one small recurring bill on it like a streaming service or your phone bill. *This should be the absolute only thing that you charge on the card.*

3. **Set up an automatic bill payment.** Go to your bank and set up an automatic payment from your bills account that will pay off the credit card balance each month. This will create a pay off loop that you can set and forget.

For this tactic to work, you must avoid swiping your card on anything else or revolving a balance. Make sure to leave this card at home to avoid temptation.

Not too hard, right?

This week we covered a ton of information on how to improve your credit score. Use the next two days to review anything that you missed!

Live Richer Challenge: Credit Edition
Day 13: Review, Reflect, Relax

Week 2: Credit Improvement

Today's Easy Financial Task: Review, Reflect, Relax

How to rock this task:
- *Review* this week's Live Richer Challenge: Credit Edition tasks
- *Reflect* on the credit basics and the components that make up your credit score
- *Relax.* In two days we start Week 3: Credit Maintenance

Hey, hey, we've made it to the end of the second week of the Live Richer Challenge: Credit Edition! Take this day to review, reflect, and relax.

Today is a great day to check in on your accountability partner(s). Do they need help with a task? Do they need some encouragement? Do you both need to catch up on past tasks?

I'd love to hear from you. You can reach out to me here:
Twitter: @thebudgetnista
Instagram: @thebudgetnista
Facebook: The Budgetnista
Private Forum: www.livericherchallenge.com
(Go to the website and request to join the private LIVE RICHER forum.)

> Don't forget: It's great to be helped, but it's even greater to use what you've been given to help someone else. Share the wealth and pass the Live Richer Challenge: Credit Edition along to someone you know who is struggling to get their credit on track.

Live Richer Challenge: Credit Edition
Day 14: Weekly Inspiration

Week 2: Credit Improvement

Today's Easy Financial Task 14: Watch the Week 2 Dream Catcher Hangout Chat.

How to rock this task:
- Watch the video
- Listen to words of encouragement
- Complete Challenge tasks you missed

Today's our second Dream Catcher Hangout Video!

During the video, we discuss the tasks we've worked on this week. We'll also talk about the key takeaways and you'll hear how other Dream Catchers like yourself work through the Challenge.

Make sure to check in on your accountability partner. Have they completed the second week of the Challenge? Are they ready for next week?

FYI: Today is a good day to catch up on any tasks that you missed throughout the week. Tomorrow, we have a fresh new week full of tasks to help you improve your credit score!

Watch the Dream Catcher Hangout at www.livericherchallenge.com
(Day 14: Weekly Inspiration)

Week 2: Credit Improvement Recap Checklist

This Week's Goal: To raise your credit score.

- **Day 8:** Credit Report Clean Up
  - ○ **Easy Financial Task:** To identify items on your credit report you can dispute.
- **Day 9:** Bills on Lock
  - ○ **Easy Financial Task:** Automate your bill payments to improve your payment history record.
- **Day 10:** Amounts Owed
  - ○ **Easy Financial Task:** Learn how to reduce the amount of debt you owe to improve your credit score.
- **Day 11:** Length of Credit History
  - ○ **Easy Financial Task:** Learn strategies to lengthen your credit history
- **Day 12:** 100 points
  - ○ **Easy Financial Task:** Learn how to make your score jump like Jordan.
- **Day 13:** Review, Reflect, Relax
  - ○ **Easy Financial Task:** Review, Reflect, Relax
- **Day 14:** Weekly Inspiration
  - ○ **Easy Financial Task:** Watch the Week 2 Dream Catcher Hangout Chat.

Week 2 Reflections

_____

_____

_____

_____

_____

_____

_____

WEEK 3: CREDIT MAINTENANCE

THIS WEEK'S GOAL:

To establish a plan for maintaining a clean credit report and high credit score over time, and to learn how to protect your credit from fraud.

Live Richer Challenge: Credit Edition
Day 15: Hard vs. Soft Inquiry

Week 3: Credit Maintenance

Today's Easy Financial Task: Learn the difference between a soft and hard credit inquiry.

How to rock this task:
- Pull out your credit report
- Review the items in the credit inquiry section of your report

Welcome to the last week of the Credit Challenge!

We're in the home stretch, Dream Catcher!

At the beginning of this Challenge, you learned the nuances of credit and what components make up your credit score.

The second week of the Challenge we focused on implementing some heavy-hitting strategies to clean up your credit report and improve your credit score.

The last piece of the puzzle is to create a game plan for:

- Keeping your credit report clean
- Maintaining credit score growth
- Protecting your credit from others

As a recap, the amount and type of credit inquiries you have on your report make up 10% of your credit score.

When you apply for a credit card, loan, rental, utilities, phone plan, and even occasionally during an employment background check, a company asks to perform a credit inquiry on you. The purpose is to check your history to make sure you're a creditworthy candidate.

You may wonder why an employer would need to review your credit report. Some companies use credit history to judge character and financial habits before hiring.

There are two types of credit inquires: soft and hard credit inquiries.

Soft Credit Inquiry (also known as a soft pull) - A soft credit inquiry is a routine check on your credit history that can happen without your permission. A soft credit inquiry does not impact your credit score.

An example of a soft inquiry is when lenders or credit card companies pre-qualify you for products before sending offers through the mail. Later this week, I'll teach you how to stop companies from pre-screening you for these credit cards and loans.

A soft pull also happens when you check your own credit history and when an employer does a background check (unless they tell you otherwise).

Hard Credit Inquiry (also known as a hard pull) - Hard inquiries are the ones that can affect your score but can only happen with your permission. Hard credit inquiries are used to make a final decision on whether or not to offer you a service, loan, or line of credit.

A bank, credit union, or company usually asks you to authorize a hard credit inquiry during the application process. If you request a credit line increase or amendment to an existing contract, a hard pull may also be required to approve the request.

A credit inquiry usually causes you to lose five or fewer points. However, if you have a short credit history or very few accounts on your report, a credit inquiry may be more impactful.

Here are three tips to follow to manage inquiries on your credit report:

1. Always ask what type of inquiry that an application will trigger.

Before you turn in a new application or request a change to one of your current accounts, double-check the type of inquiry it will cause.

2. Shop for loans with a plan.

You should always compare rates with multiple lenders to get the best deal before taking out a new auto loan, student loan, mortgage, or personal loan.

The good news is, if you are shopping for a car or home loan, several lenders can pull your credit within a 30 to 45 day window while you shop around for the best interest rate and terms. The multiple inquiries will have the impact of just one hard inquiry.

Use this to your advantage. Make a list of lenders that you want to compare prices with first. Then, submit your applications back-to-back to be strategic with your hard credit inquiries.

3. Don't apply for any and every credit card.

Multiple hard inquiries for credit cards are not viewed the same as shopping for a loan. If you apply for many credit cards, it's looked at as a sign you may be experiencing some money trouble.

Don't get enticed by the credit card sign up discounts at the retail counter either. Applying for each credit card will require a hard pull on your report.

Before we close today's task, I want you to circle back to your credit report to review the hard credit inquiries on it.

Ask yourself these questions:

- What applications or activities triggered a hard pull on my credit?
- Do I apply for accounts that I don't need?
- How can I avoid/limit inquiries in the future?

That brings us to the end of today's task Dream Catcher!

Live Richer Challenge: Credit Edition
Day 16: Your Credit Mix

Week 3: Credit Maintenance

Today's Easy Financial Task: Learn about the type of debt that makes up your credit mix and what to consider before taking on new debt.

How to rock this task:
- Pull out your credit report
- Review the types of debt you have
- Learn how to decide when it's the right time to open a new account

Hey, there! Welcome to Day 16 of the Challenge, Dream Catcher.

Today's a video day! *Happy Dance*

Watch the video of me explaining today's task and come back and get to work. You can find video at www.livericherchallenge.com under the book resources tab (Day 16: Your Credit Mix).

In today's task, we're talking about your credit mix. For a quick reminder, your credit mix is the different types of debt you have on your credit report.

Although credit mix makes up only 10% of your credit score, financial institutions like to see a mix of both revolving and installment accounts on your credit report because it shows you have a history of managing various forms of debt.

Examples of revolving accounts are credit cards, retail accounts, and any other account where you're only required to pay a minimum amount each month and you can revolve the remaining balance to the next billing cycle.

Examples of installment loans are auto loans, personal loans, and mortgages. These are loans with a preset loan term that you make scheduled payments on each month.

If your credit report lacks one type of debt (revolving accounts or installment loans), you may be wondering if you should open another account to improve your credit mix.

Although diversity is good, it's important to understand:

You shouldn't open an account just for the sake of opening an account.

Instead, diversify your accounts over time and only as necessary. Before opening a new account, ask yourself a few key questions:

Do I need it?

Only open accounts that:

- Serve a purpose
- You're committed to managing responsibly
- You can afford

If you're building credit from scratch, before opening a line of credit make sure that you trust yourself to spend within your means and that you can keep up with payments. Otherwise, opening an account before you're ready can do more harm than good.

One company I highly recommend (again), is Self Lender. You can read my full review and learn more about how they work, at www.livericherchallenge.com (Day 11: Length of Credit History)

Also, remember the "Jump like Jordan" tactic of putting a small balance on a credit card and paying it off entirely each month (from the Day 12 task) can increase your score as much as 100 points in a year too.

However, this will only work if you have enough discipline to keep the credit card balance low so you can pay it back in full each billing cycle.

What will a new account do to my credit history length?

Remember, your credit history length is an average, so opening new accounts will shorten your credit history length overall.

Tip: When you do open a new account, don't close any of your old revolving accounts even if they have negative records like late payments. The late payments will stay on your history and impact your score whether the account is open or closed, but the account age can still do positive things for your credit history length.

Have I done my homework on the account that I'm considering?

Choose your accounts carefully. Even though some retail credit cards and store financing options are easy to qualify for, they can also have a higher interest rate than a major credit card. I suggest staying far away from retail/store cards.

Before opening an account confirm:
- The interest rate and compare it to other credit cards, loans, or financing offers
- The fees and compare it to other credit cards, loans, or financing offers
- What credit bureaus the credit card or loan issuer reports to
- That there is no additional fine print to the credit card or financing contract you need to be aware of.

Take a moment to review your current credit mix.

What accounts do you currently have?

What accounts do you plan on adding in the future that will diversify your mix?

To make your life easier, Credit Sesame has a section of your online credit report where you can review your credit mix. Get a special Dream Catcher link for Credit Sesame at www.livericherchallenge.com, under the book resources tab (Day 2: Credit Basics).

When you sign-up, Credit Sesame will extend to you, up to $50,000 worth of identity theft Insurance, for free. Yup!

My current credit mix is....

_____

_____

_____

_____

_____

_____

_____

_____

_____

_____

_____

Live Richer Challenge: Credit Edition
Day 17: Lower Interest Rates

Week 3: Credit Maintenance

Today's Easy Financial Task: Lower your interest rates.

How to Rock This Task:
- Learn how to use a balance transfer to lower your interest rate
- Learn how to use an installment loan to lower your interest rate

Hey there, Dream Catcher! A new day, a new task.

Last week, one of our tasks was creating a debt repayment plan. The amount of debt you owe makes up 30% of your credit score, so lowering your debt can do great things for your credit.

During that task, I mentioned this week we would discuss ways to reduce your interest rate while paying off debt. That day has come!

Did you fill out the My Debt List from Day 10? If not, do so now. I've created a My Debt List spreadsheet that you can access for free at www.livericher-challenge.com under the book resources tab (Day 10: Amounts Owed). You can also find it at the end of today's task.

Now let's get to work...

There are two options for lowering your interest rate:

Option #1: You can transfer your balance from one credit card to another card that's offering a sign on deal. This is called a credit card balance transfer.

Option #2: You can take out a personal loan with a lower interest rate to consolidate your credit card debt.

(If you do decide to do a balance transfer or take out a personal loan, **don't cancel the original card.** Keep it open because it's contributing to your credit history length.)

How to Find a Balance Transfer Card

1. Go to MagnifyMoney.com to search for a balance transfer card that offers 0% interest for at least six months and has the lowest balance transfer fee.

Some credit card companies offer 0% introductory interest and no balance transfer fee - that's ideal. A balance transfer fee of more than 3% is too high.

2. When you find a card, make sure you understand from the term online:
    a. The 0% APR introductory period
    b. What the rate will be after the introductory period expires
    c. The balance transfer fee
    d. What happens if you make a late payment (for some credit cards the introductory period will end abruptly, and you'll even be charged penalty interest indefinitely if you pay late)
    e. How much of your balance is likely to be transferred. They may or may not transfer it all.
    f. That there isn't any additional fine print

3. Once you're satisfied with the balance transfer terms, apply for the credit card. Once you receive the credit card, call the number on the back of the card to speak with a representative about transferring your credit card balance.

The information you need to do the balance transfer is your original credit card account number and the balance you want to move.

How to Apply for an Installment Loan

We talked about using an installment loan to reduce the amount of debt you owe in Day 10, but it's worth mentioning again here. Besides reducing your credit utilization, an installment loan is also a good way to reduce your interest rate.

If you qualify for an installment loan with a competitive interest rate, you can use the funds from the loan to pay off your credit card debt. Then, you make monthly payments on the loan until it's paid off.

Here's a refresher on how to find an installment loan:

1. Go to www.livericherchallenge.com, under the book resources tab (Day 17: Lower Interest Rates), to use our special Dream Catcher link to search for a personal loan that has low fees and a lower interest rate than your credit cards.

2. When you find a personal loan that has favorable terms, call the lender to confirm:
   a. The loan interest rate
   b. If there are any application or processing fees
   c. How long the loan term is
   d. Whether applying for the loan will trigger a hard inquiry on your report
   e. If there are any fine print or other fees you should be aware of

Important Tip: Factors that determine the full cost of an installment loan include the interest rate, fees, your monthly payment, *and* how long the loan term is.

Make sure to ask how much you'll pay in interest for the **entire** loan term to find an installment loan that will save you the most money.

Ready, set, go ahead and get cracking on today's task!

Transferring a balance and applying for an installment loan the first time can be intimidating, so feel free to reach out to your accountability partners(s) for support.

You can also reach out to our group in the Dream Catcher Forum found at www.livericherchallenge.com. (Go to the website and request to join the private LIVE RICHER forum.)

My Debt List
(NOTE: List debt lowest to highest)

NAME OF DEBT	TOTAL AMT. OWED	MIN. MONTHLY PMT.	INTEREST RATE	DUE DATE	STATUS

Live Richer Challenge: Credit Edition
Day 18: Relationships and Credit

Week 3: Credit Maintenance

Today's Easy Financial Task: Learn how to respond to family and friends who want you to cosign for their loan or who take advantage of your credit.

How to Rock This Task:
- Respond to family and friends who ask to use your credit for their gain
- Remove yourself as a cosigner from someone else's loan
- Remove authorized users from your credit card accounts

We're back!

There are just a few more days left in this Challenge, but many more tasks to cover, so roll up your sleeves, folks!

This week our mission is establishing a game plan for long-term credit maintenance. We can't cover this topic without getting serious about how relationships can impact our credit.

Let's just be real here: When you experience financial abundance whether it's career growth, wealth, or a good credit score, people around you notice, and some will ask for favors.

There's nothing wrong with sharing wealth or abundance. In fact, giving back activates abundance in your life. However, when your credit is at stake, you need to make sure these favors won't be detrimental to your family's financial future.

Be cautious of co-signing or giving someone access to your credit.

Here's why:
If you cosign on a loan or credit card for someone who doesn't pay, the history will appear on your credit report and, even worse, you're also on the hook for the debt.

A family member or friend who asks you to cosign for them may appear to have a stable source of income and intentions to pay up, but there's no way to know for certain what the future holds. Things happen (i.e. medical emergencies or job loss) that can impact their ability to pay.

Furthermore, when you give someone free reign to use your credit cards, you're the one responsible for repaying that debt on time. The child, partner, relative, or friend, is not facing the repercussions of the unpaid debt on your credit history.

Having conversations with loved ones about favors that involve cosigning or access to your credit lines is challenging. No one wants to be that sister, cousin, mom, or aunt who's tight with purse strings.

However, in this instance, it's your right to say "no."

Since it's a tough conversation to have, here are angles to approach the situation and scripts you can use. Just fill in the name of who you're talking to in the blanks.

If someone asks you to cosign on their student loan, mortgage, personal loan, auto loan, credit card, etc.:

Approach #1: I want to support you, but I also need to hear your plan first.

"_____ (their name), I admire your ambition and desire to go to school. How much will you need in a loan? What are you studying and what is the career/salary growth within that field? What is your plan for paying it back? For me even to consider co-signing _____ (son/daughter), I need to feel confident in your career plans. "

Approach #2: I'm in the process of building credit and can't help at this time.

"Sorry, _____(their name), I'm working on my credit to buy my own _____ (house, car, boat, etc.) and cosigning is another responsibility that doesn't fit into the plan right now."

Approach #3: I don't mix money and relationships.

"Sorry, _____ (their name), I have a rule that I never cosign for anyone. It's nothing personal; I just like to keep my relationships and finances separate. Money disputes can be real relationship killers."

Approach #4: Straightforward

"Sorry, _____ (their name), cosigning makes me also financially responsible for the loan. If something should happen and you can't make payments, I would have to take ownership of the debt. I don't feel comfortable assuming this responsibility."

If someone asks to use your credit card:

Approach #1: Cut to the chase.

"Sorry,_____(their name), I currently don't have the funds."

Approach #2: I have other financial goals.

"Sorry,_____(their name), I'm working on aggressively repaying my current debt. I want to be debt free by _____, so I can't let you use my credit card."

Approach #3: I'm using cash only right now.

"Sorry,_____(their name), I'm on a cash only spending kick, so I can't give you my credit card for _____."

What if you've already said yes to a favor?

Hindsight is always 20/20, right?

You may be regretting that you agreed to cosign on a loan or that you currently allow a child, partner, or relative to paint the town with your credit card.

There are some ways to get out of it:

Sell or pay off the loan - If the borrower can't keep up with the loan payment, it may be time for them to cut their losses and sell the car or whatever asset it is they can no longer make payments on.

Although it's not the best (or most affordable) scenario, you could also bite the bullet and pay the loan off yourself to stop the borrower's poor payment history from damaging your credit.

Apply for cosigner release - Cosigner release can be an option if the loan you're a cosigner on is in good standing. Once a certain amount of consecutive, on-time payments are made on a loan, the borrower may qualify to have you removed from the contract.

Cosigner release may be available for both federal and private student loans. Reach out to your loan servicer for details.

Refinance the loan - A loan refinance is when you take out a new loan with better terms to repay another loan. Having the borrower apply for a refinance on their own is another way to get your name off of the contract.

Remove authorized users from your cards - If someone you added as an authorized user on your credit card account is overstepping boundaries, you can cut them off by contacting your credit card company to have them removed.

If someone you know is using your credit card without asking, you can also file a dispute on their charges and request a new card. Many credit cards have a zero liability policy which means you aren't held responsible for unauthorized charges when your card is lost or stolen. Check with your credit card issuer for details.

If you're stuck cosigning on someone else's loan or someone is abusing your credit, don't be too hard on yourself. Consider it a lesson learned and avoid cosigning or being lax with your credit cards in the future.

Navigating relationships, money, and credit is never easy. So, reach out to your fellow Dream Catchers participating in the Challenge if you need another perspective on how to address your situation.

Use this section to create your own script.

Live Richer Challenge: Credit Edition
Day 19: Scams and Fraud

Week 3: Credit Maintenance

Today's Easy Financial Task: Protect your identity and credit from scams and fraud.

How to rock this task:
- Set up a fraud alert or credit freeze if necessary
- Use optoutprescreen.com to opt out of credit card and insurance pre-approval offers to gain control of who gets access to your credit history

Welcome to Day 19!

The purpose of today's task is to make sure that you remain vigilant. Technology is always evolving, so it's easier than ever for scammers to get access to your personal information and use it for their financial gain.

Fortunately, you can take steps to limit the chances of your identity getting stolen and minimize the damage a scammer can do to your credit if you suspect identity theft.

Here are a few ways to protect yourself:

Never save your login information: Many websites give the option to save your username and password for the next time you log in. Never save this information. If someone untrustworthy gets their hands on your device, they get an all access pass to your entire life.

Don't use the same username and password for all of your accounts. This includes email, social media, bank, and credit card accounts. If someone figures out how to get into one account, they have access to each one.

Don't share personal information through email: Emails can get intercepted and networks can get hacked, so avoid using it to exchange sensitive information.

Sign up for credit monitoring: Always monitor your credit report to catch inconsistencies right away to minimize the impact of identity theft if it does happen.

Remember, you're entitled to a free credit report from each credit bureau annually. (For a refresher on where you can get your credit report for free, go back to Day 3.)

You can sign up for FREE credit monitoring with Credit Sesame. Get a special Dream Catcher link for Credit Sesame at www.livericherchallenge.com, under the book resources tab (Day 2: Credit Basics).

Set up fraud alerts: If you suspect someone has stolen your identity or someone is misusing your personal information, you can set up fraud alerts with the credit bureaus.

When a fraud alert is activated, a company has to take the extra step of double-checking your identity when an application is received before offering credit. This extra verification step can make it harder for a scammer to commit fraud in your name.

An initial fraud alert lasts for 90 days and is free to set up. Once the 90 days end, you have the option to renew the fraud alert. You can set up fraud alerts here:

- Experian Fraud Alert
- Equifax Fraud Alert
- TransUnion Fraud Alert

Set up a credit freeze (or security freeze): Credit freezing is another layer of security that's even tighter than a fraud alert. Credit freezing locks your credit report entirely.

To allow a company, employer, or financial institution to pull a report, you'll have to temporarily lift the credit freeze. Unlike the fraud alerts, credit freezing and unfreezing may cost you between $3 and $10 depending on your state. You can set up credit freezes here:

- Experian Credit Freeze
- TransUnion Credit Freeze
- Equifax Credit Freeze

Monitor your bank and credit card accounts: Besides keeping an eye out for new accounts taken out in your name, you should be mindful of your existing accounts as well. Review your bank and credit card statements to pick up on unfamiliar charges.

Sign up for up to $50,000 in FREE identity theft insurance: Use Credit Sesame. Again, when you sign up for Credit Sesame's free credit monitoring, they'll automatically give you $50,000 identity theft insurance, plus live access to talk to identity restoration specialists — for freeeeeeee.

Note: You can find all of these links in a clickable format at www.livericherchallenge.com under the book resources tab. (Day 19: Scams and Fraud)

Opt-Out of Unwarranted Prescreens from Credit Card and Insurance Companies

We briefly discussed how credit card and insurance companies might pre-qualify you for products without you knowing. I also mentioned there's a way to opt-out of these pre-screenings.

Remember, these offers don't impact your credit score since it's a soft pull on your credit, but they can be nuisance junk mail. Plus, you don't want the offers to get in the wrong hands. You are entitled to opt-out of these screenings to limit junk mail and to unlist yourself from company databases.

You can do so for free at www.optoutprescreen.com. Opting out of the list lasts for five years or you can choose to do it permanently.

In today's task, we covered many ways to protect your identity and I can't stress enough the importance of staying cautious. Going through credit and identity repair after fraud is a long and challenging process. Do what you can now to prevent it from happening.

As a recap, here are the actions you can take right now to protect your identity:

1. Go to each of the websites where you manage your financial accounts online and remove the saved username and password.

2. Switch up your username and passwords so they're not all the same. Write down your username and passwords and keep them somewhere safe.

3. Set fraud alerts or credit freezes on your account if you're in a situation now where you believe someone may have access to your private information.

4. Sign up for Identity Protection

5. Opt-out of company pre-screens if you want to stop getting preapproved for products.

That's a wrap for today's task.

Liver Richer Challenge: Credit Edition
Day 20: Review, Reflect, Relax

Week 3: Credit Maintenance

Today's Easy Financial Task: Review, Reflect, Relax

How to rock this task:
- *Review* this week's Live Richer Challenge: Credit Edition tasks
- *Reflect* on the credit maintenance tasks
- *Relax*. You're almost done!

Hey, hey, we've made it to the end of the third week of the Live Richer Challenge: Credit Edition! Take this day to review, reflect, and relax.

Today is a great day to check in on your accountability partner(s). Do they need help with a task? Do they need some encouragement? Do you both need to catch up on past tasks?

I'd love to hear from you. You can reach out to me here:

Twitter: @thebudgetnista
Instagram: @thebudgetnista
Facebook: The Budgetnista
Private Forum: www.livericherchallenge.com
(Go to the website and request to join the private LIVE RICHER forum.)

Don't forget: It's great to be helped, but it's even greater to use what you've been given to help someone else. Share the wealth and pass the Live Richer Challenge: Credit Edition along to someone you know who is struggling to master their credit.

Live Richer Challenge: Credit Edition
Day 21: Weekly Inspiration

Week 3: Credit Maintenance

Today's Easy Financial Task: Watch the Week 3 Dream Catcher Hangout Chat.

How to Rock This Task:
- Watch the chat
- Listen to words of encouragement
- Complete Challenge tasks you missed

Today's our final Dream Catcher Hangout!

During the video, we'll discuss the tasks we've worked on this week. We'll also talk about the key takeaways and you'll hear how other Dream Catchers like yourself work through the Challenge.

Make sure to check in on your accountability partner. Have they completed the first and second weeks of the Challenge?

FYI: Today is a good day to catch up on any tasks that you missed throughout the week.

Watch the Dream Catcher Hangout at www.livericherchallenge.com (Day 21: Weekly Inspiration)

DAY 22: LIVE RICHER

FINAL DAY'S GOAL:

To learn how to purposefully and passionately pursue an abundant life by using your finances (credit) as one of your tools.

Live Richer Challenge: Credit Edition
Day 22: Credit Increase Aspirations

Week 3: LIVE RICHER

Today's Easy Financial Task: Write down the steps you've taken so far to increase your credit score and chart your progress.

How to rock this task:
- Circle back to your Day 1 credit score goals
- Write down each action you took (or plan to take) to increase your score on your Credit Goal Sheet from Day 1.
- Chart your progress on the Credit Goal Sheet
- Visualize what you'll obtain when you reach your credit score goal

You've made it to the end of the LRC: Credit Challenge!

Give yourself a hand clap!

At the beginning of this Challenge, you wrote down your credit goals.

Since then, as promised, we've covered a bunch of actions you can take to make this goal happen.

If you haven't already, head back to your goal sheet and write down each action step that you've taken or plan to take consistently to turn your goal into reality. You can find the goal sheet at www.livericherchallenge.com under the book resources tab (Day 1: Credit Goals).

As you work towards your goals, use the Credit Goal handout from Day 1 to track your progress. This is an important step. Your credit score can fluctuate from month-to-month as you pay off debt and make other moves. You need to make sure your credit score is always trending upwards.

The very last task for our Challenge is imagining what you want to do with your newly increased credit score.

Why?

Your credit score is an important number. But like money, it's just a tool to get the things you want in life.

Think about what you want to achieve with a higher credit score so that you can associate an image with the score.

- Do you want to buy a new house?
- Do you want to buy a rental property?
- Do you want to refinance your auto loan to get a better interest rate?
- Do you want to get approved for your first apartment without a cosigner?

Think of why you want to increase your score and then do these three things:

1. Comment what you will obtain with your higher credit score in the comments of the LRC: Credit Challenge thread in the Dream Catchers Forum
2. Write down what you aspire to obtain with your higher credit score on the Credit Goal handout to keep for yourself
3. Find a photo that represents what you want to obtain and post it on your fridge

Get to it!

Once you're finished with these tasks, you've officially completed the LRC: Credit Challenge.

Let me hear your wins. If you've tackled any of the tasks in this Challenge and have already seen a credit score increase, I want to know!

You can reach out to me using social media below.
Thank you for participating. You're a rockstar and truly a Dream Catcher!
Twitter: @thebudgetnista
Instagram: @thebudgetnista
Facebook: The Budgetnista
Private Forum: www.livericherchallenge.com
(Go to the website and request to join the private LIVE RICHER forum.)

Week 3: Credit Maintenance Recap Checklist

This Week's Goal: To establish a plan for maintaining a clean credit report and high credit score over time. To learn how to protect your credit from fraudsters.

- **Day 15:** Hard vs. Soft Inquiry
    - ○ **Easy Financial Task:** Learn the difference between a soft and hard credit inquiry.

- **Day 16:** Your Credit Mix
    - ○ **Easy Financial Task:** Learn about the type of debt that makes up your credit mix and what to consider before taking on new debt.

- **Day 17:** Lower Interest Rates
    - ○ **Easy Financial Task:** Lower your interest rates.

- **Day 18:** Relationships and Credit
    - ○ **Easy Financial Task:** Learn how to respond to family and friends who want you to cosign for their loan or who take advantage of your credit.

- **Day 19:** Scams and Fraud
    - ○ **Easy Financial Task:** Protect your identity and credit from scams and fraud

- **Day 20:** Review, Reflect, Relax
    - ○ **Easy Financial Task:** Review, Reflect, Relax

- **Day 21:** Weekly Inspiration
    - ○ **Easy Financial Task:** Watch the Week 2 Dream Catcher Hangout Chat.

- **Day 22:** Credit Increase Aspirations
    - ○ **Easy Financial Task:** Chart your credit score increases and write down what you want to obtain when your credit score reaches your goal.

LIVE RICHER Challenge Reflections

Acknowledgments:

First and foremost, I would like to give my most grateful thanks to God. He always blesses us. It is we who allow or do not allow our blessings to manifest.

I also want to thank Mommy, Daddy, and my sisters: Karen, Tracy, Carol, and Lisa. You are my cheerleaders, my best friends, my sounding board, and my inspiration. Anyone who knows the Aliche Girls knows how supportive we are of each other. Thank you.

To all my family, both here and abroad, thank you for your constant love and support. The strong foundation you've provided is the reason I've been able to reach such heights.

Taylor Medine and Maria, thank you so much for helping me transform and polish my words into a book I can be proud of.

Superman a.k.a. Jerrell, thank you for your unwavering support and love.

Thank you to my designer Hector Torres. I came to you at crunch time and you more than delivered.

Thank you, Sierra Kirby. I literally could not have launched the LIVE RICHER Challenge without you.

Jubril Agoro, thank you for helping me to amplify my voice.

Special thanks to Linda Iferika, Dreena Whitfield, all my family, friends, coworkers, and all of my well wishers.

Lastly, I especially want to thank you. Yes, you reading these words. You allowed me to help you LIVE RICHER. You gave me more than I ever gave you. I am forever grateful.

Tiffany "The Budgetnista" Aliche is an award-winning teacher of financial empowerment and is quickly becoming America's favorite financial educator. The Budgetnista specializes in the delivery of financial literacy and has served as the personal finance education expert for City National Bank.

Since 2008, The Budgetnista has been a brand ambassador and spokesperson for a number of organizations, delivering financial education through seminars, workshops, curricula and trainings. In 2014, Tiffany founded the LIVE RICHER Challenge Movement, a virtual community of hundreds of thousands of women from 50 states and 100+ countries.

Author of #1 Amazon bestseller The One Week Budget and Live Richer Challenge, Tiffany and her financial advice have been featured in The New York Times, Reuters, US News and World Report, Good Morning America, The TODAY Show, PBS, Fox Business, MSNBC, CBS Money-Watch, TIME, ESSENCE Magazine, and FORBES. She regularly blogs about personal finance for The Huffington Post and U.S. News and World Report and Black Enterprise

You can learn more about Tiffany and The Budgetnista at www.thebudgetnista.com.

Made in the USA
Columbia, SC
08 June 2020